# DRAWN

### AND

# QUARTERED

# PAUL CONRAD
## THE BEST POLITICAL CARTOONS

TEXTS BY
### RICHARD C. BERGHOLZ

INTRODUCTION BY
### WILLIAM F. THOMAS
EDITOR AND
EXECUTIVE
VICE PRESIDENT
*LOS ANGELES TIMES*

# DRAWN AND QUARTERED

"I'VE NEVER WORN MAKEUP."

**HARRY N. ABRAMS, INC., PUBLISHERS, NEW YORK**

*To my wife, Kay*

Project Director: Robert Morton
Designer: Michael Hentges

**Library of Congress Cataloging in Publication Data**

Conrad, Paul, 1924–
    Los Angeles times drawn and quartered.

    I. United States—Politics and government—1981–
—Caricatures and cartoons. 2. American wit and humor,
Pictorial. I. Bergholz, Richard C., 1917–
II. Los Angeles times. III. Title.
E876.C67 1985    741.5′092′4    85–7332
ISBN 0–8109–1291–0

Published in 1985 by Harry N. Abrams, Incorporated, New York

Printed and bound in the United States of America

# C O N T E N T S

# INTRODUCTION

Every so often, particularly at election time, I am compelled to try to explain Paul Conrad. And the cartoonist's role. I do so usually, let's say almost always, in response to letters with phrases like "the last straw" and whose ultimate sentence contains the word "cancel."

Friends seldom write; critics do.

I've been trying to explain Conrad for fourteen years, but never satisfactorily. The reason for this, I suspect, is that his art, and with Conrad we are talking about art, is visceral. You *feel* it, you don't rationalize it. In fact, as he and I have sometimes agreed, if you have to explain a cartoon the thing didn't work.

That said, I'm going to explain Paul Conrad anyway—from my point of view.

I consider Conrad a great cartoonist. My criteria include effectiveness and power, and a style and a message to arouse a rush of strong emotion. He is one of the few remaining cartoonists of his genre, a genre that aims the most powerful and unambiguous punch it can muster straight for the heart.

Many of today's cartoonists tend to rely on a more subtle approach, and many of them are very good indeed. But they are not Paul Conrad.

Conrad is about as subtle as a rocket launch. He fully intends to hit as hard as he can, and he has no doubts whatever about the unassailable truth of his message, its *rightness*. There are for him no shades of gray, and he worries not one whit about the qualifications and ambiguities that you and I factor into our judgments.

We are trying to be fair; great cartoonists never are.

For they approach a subject much as a child would, stripping it of distractions, reducing it to its simplest and purest elements. Then, if like Conrad they possess the artist's tools to pull it off, they frame the message in bold black strokes—often outrageous, funny, sometimes sad, always unmistakable.

Very few of us could bring ourselves to view the world in such stark terms, and there is little doubt that genuine anguish has been felt by those whose convictions are deeply offended by such judgments. I have the letters to prove it, and it is impossible for anyone not to sympathize with those whose own deeply held views are sometimes treated, it's fair to say, harshly.

One tries to explain that no newspaper views the cartoonist's latitude as boundless; even Conrad must abide by certain guidelines.

But it is necessary to explain at the same time that the message being conveyed usually is not essentially different from those expounded in newspaper opinion columns, and that it would thus be illogical to forbid the cartoonist his message simply because the manner of conveyance is different—profoundly different.

This Conrad collection shows his many facets, ranging from the sadly sentimental farewells to Jimmy Durante and Hubert Humphrey to the risqué nude of the Statue of Liberty to the brutal depiction of the Watergate Haldeman as "Son of Nixonstein." His messages are simple but his interests are broad and, as you'll see here, sometimes surprising.

It's been a real trial on occasion to have been editor of the *Times* through fourteen years of Conrad, but it's been a rare treat, too. For Conrad is the best there is.

WILLIAM F. THOMAS
Editor and Executive Vice President
*Los Angeles Times*

# THIS LAND IS YOUR LAND,
# THIS LAND IS MY LAND

"THE ENVIRONMENTAL EXTREMISTS WON'T BE SATISFIED UNTIL THE WHITE HOUSE LOOKS LIKE A BIRD'S NEST!"

"WELL, THERE GOES THE NEIGHBORHOOD..."

There can be humor in adversity, as in this Conrad comment on the forced evacuation of the city of Times Beach, Missouri, where a dump of toxic contaminants was discovered.

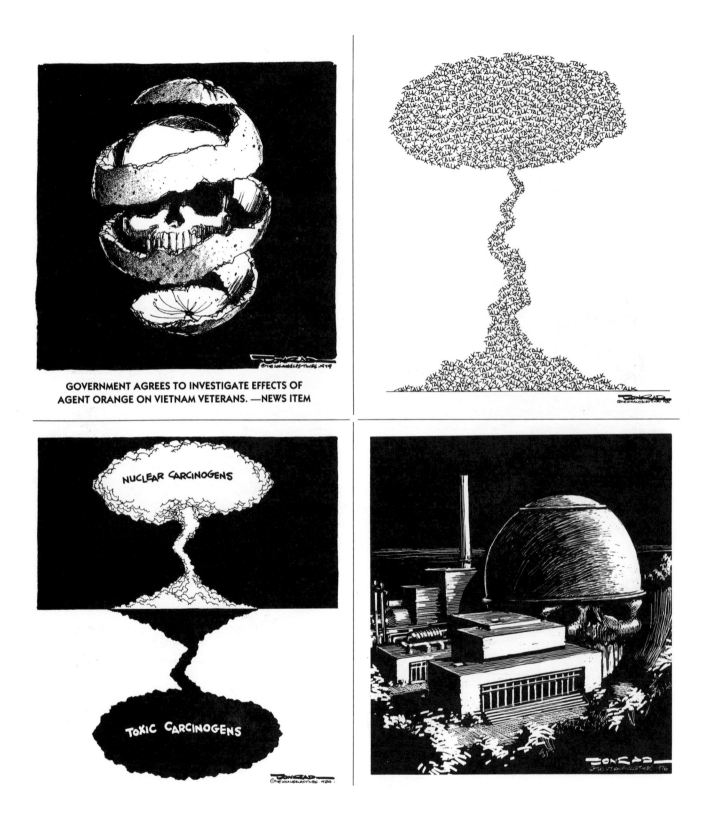

GOVERNMENT AGREES TO INVESTIGATE EFFECTS OF
AGENT ORANGE ON VIETNAM VETERANS. —NEWS ITEM

"THERE'S NO WASTE PROBLEM...WE JUST DIG A NEW HOLE!"

"OK, WHO TURNED OFF THE POWER...?"

STILL LIFE

"I'M NOBODY'S PUPPET!"

Miss Piggy of the Muppets was the foil for commenting on Rita Lavelle's denial of her involvement in the Environmental Protection Agency's lack of response to toxic waste problems.

ENVIRONMENTAL PRIMER FOR WILLIAM CLARK

"TOMORROW, TOMORROW,
WE'LL CLEAN UP TOMORROW,
WE'RE ONLY THE E PA !"

"ANNE CAN STAY ON AS LONG AS SHE WISHES."

"ANNE CAN WALK OUT OF THE EPA WITH HER HEAD HELD HIGH!"

WATT REMOVES AGENCY LAND FROM SALES PLAN. —NEWS ITEM

WATT MAN

BUREAU OF LAND MANAGEMENT'S LAND MANAGEMENT PLAN

## LORD OF THE FLIES

When Governor Jerry Brown delayed aerial spraying for Mediterranean fruit flies, Conrad called up the title of William Golding's famous book to dramatize the issue.

Howls of protest from Northern California followed this cartoon after the north's 95% rejection of a California ballot initiative that would have provided more upstate water for central and Southern California.

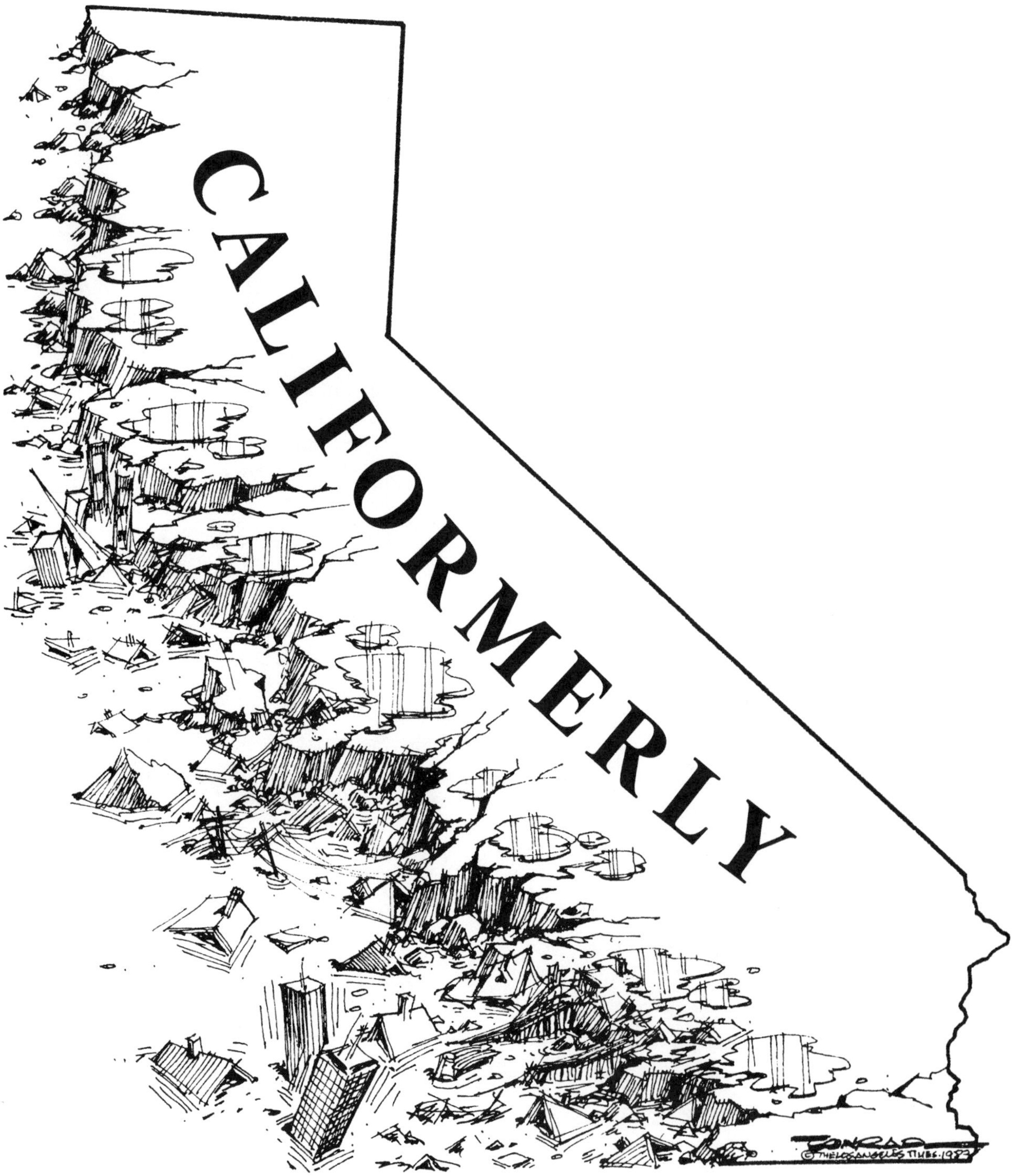
CALIFORMERLY
CONRAD
© THE LOS ANGELES TIMES 1983

**HEAD OF THE MEDUSA**

"THAR SHE BLOWS!"

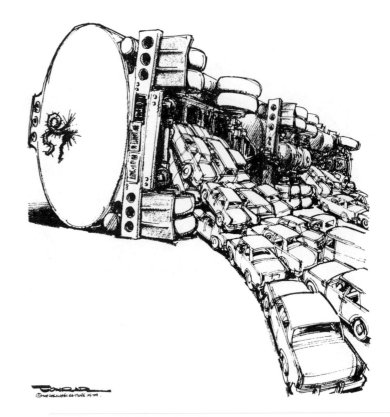

"WE ARE HOLDING THE NORTHEAST HOSTAGE! DEREGULATE NATURAL GAS OR THEY FREEZE!"

CALIFORNIA SYNDROME

MICROSCOPIC VIEW OF BACTERIA DEVELOPED TO EAT OIL

Conrad's version of a scientist's plan to use bacteria to absorb oil spills reveals the true shape of that microbe.

"WHAT'S SO TERRIBLE ABOUT 'BLACK LUNG'...?"

# HAIL TO THE CHIEFS

**THE KING IS DEAD...LONG LIVE THE PRESIDENCY!**

"ERA OF RECONCILIATION"

"HE SAYS HE'S FROM THE PHONE COMPANY..."

PRESIDENT ABSORBED IN BIOGRAPHY OF NAPOLEON. —NEWS ITEM

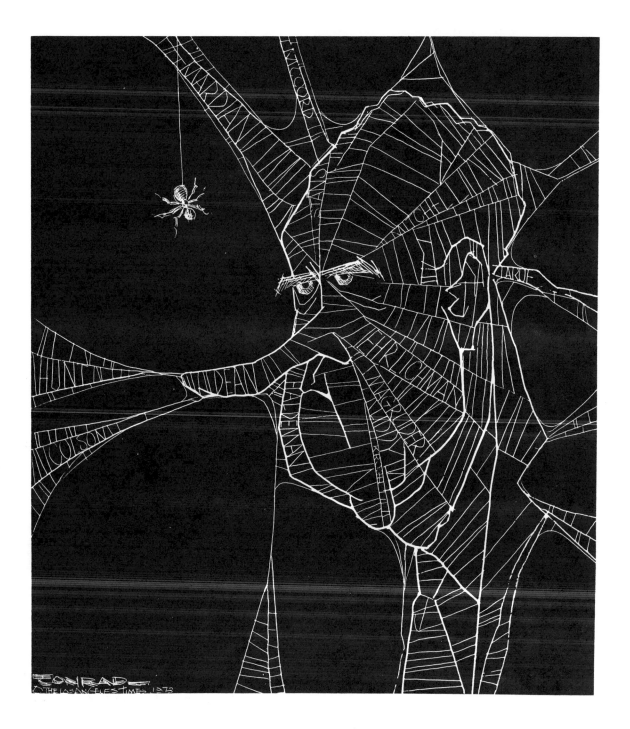

THE AGONY AND THE ECSTASY

The financial windfall from paid TV interviews and book contracts that came to former President Nixon, thus capitalizing on his role in the national disgrace of Watergate, was particularly galling to Conrad.

CONRAD
© THE LOS ANGELES TIMES, 1977

ONE FLEW OVER THE CUCKOO'S NEST

THE GETAWAY CAR

An Oscar-winning 1976 film best described for Conrad the second anniversary of Nixon's dramatic exit from the White House.

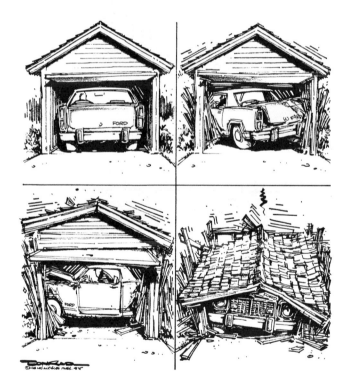

TURNING THE ECONOMY AROUND

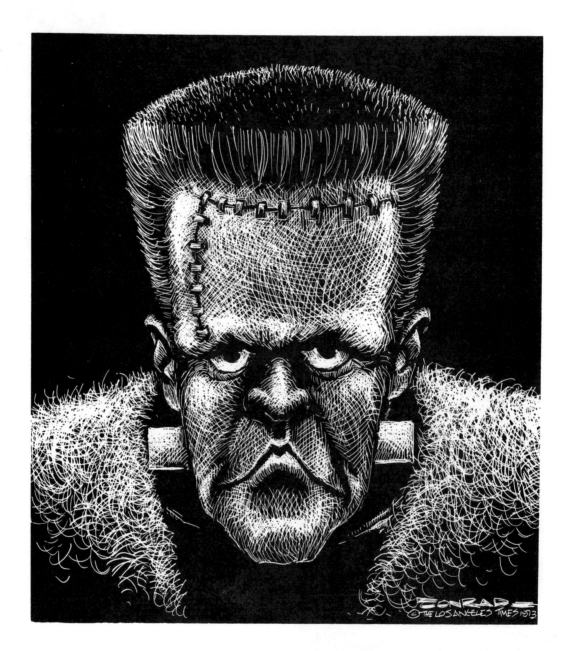

SON OF NIXONSTEIN

"MY OPPONENT IS DELIBERATELY DISTORTING MY POSITION!"

"WELL! I'VE OFTEN SEEN A CAT WITHOUT A GRIN," THOUGHT ALICE; "BUT
A GRIN WITHOUT A CAT! IT'S THE MOST CURIOUS THING I EVER SAW!"

Jimmy Carter's admission in the 1976 campaign that he sometimes "lusted in his heart" provoked this example of the Conrad wit.

"ANOTHER FINE MESS YOU'VE GOTTEN US INTO, OLLIE..."

"DO I HEAR $225,000...?"

Brother Billy provided yet another problem for President Carter with the disclosure that during the 1980 campaign Billy had been paid fat fees by Arab interests to lobby for them.

REQUIEM FOR A LIGHTWEIGHT

RESCUE MISSION

"NOW THAT THE ISSUES HAVE BECOME MORE MANAGEABLE..."

"WILL THERE BE ANY JEWS AT ANWAR'S FUNERAL?"

This old schoolboy trick best described Conrad's view of John Anderson's role in the 1980 campaign.

"HE COMES IN EVERY DAY...SLAMS A FEW DOORS...KICKS A FEW TIRES..."

"I PICK MY ARROWS OUT OF THIN AIR..."

"HAVEN'T WE MET BEFORE? DO YOU COME HERE OFTEN? CAN I BUY
YOU A DRINK? HOW ABOUT A SEAT ON THE U.S. SUPREME COURT?"

"I'VE BEEN SUPPORTING REAGAN FOR OVER 40 YEARS!"

A typical Conrad twist on Reagan's frequent defense of his movie role opposite the chimp Bonzo provided this zinger.

"<u>NOT</u> ON THE NEWSPAPERS!"

"NANCY, I GOT THE PART!"

A PAGE OUT OF PRESIDENT REAGAN'S MAKE-UP MAN'S SKETCHBOOK

"...EVEN THE LOS ANGELES TIMES GIVES YOU A RAVE REVIEW!"

"TAKE OFF THAT STUPID BUTTON!"

"BY GOLLY, GEE WHIZ, IT'S SURE GOOD TO SERVE THIS PRESIDENT!"

OFFICIAL INAUGURAL PORTRAIT

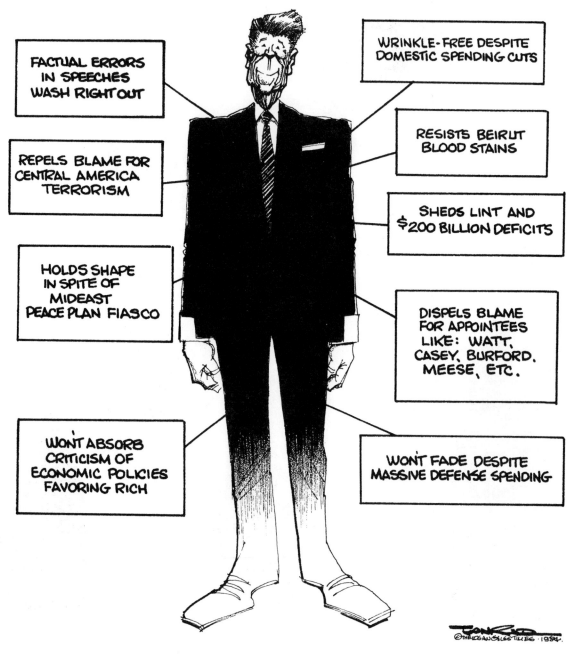

THE MAN IN THE TEFLON-COATED SUIT

"WHERE DID WE GO WRONG?"

VAST WORLDWIDE MISINFORMATION MACHINE

LANDSLIDE

"OTHER THAN YOUR FRIENDSHIP WITH THE PRESIDENT,
MR. BONZO, WHAT QUALIFIES YOU FOR THIS CABINET POSITION?"

"TO THE PRESIDENT! WHO IS MAKING EVEN US LOOK GOOD!"

"REDISTRICT THIS STATE REPUBLICAN OR ELSE...!"

Governor Deukmejian's frantic defense of a California Republican-sponsored initiative to wrest control of some districts from Democrats elicited this response.

"NOW, ABOUT THE RULES..."

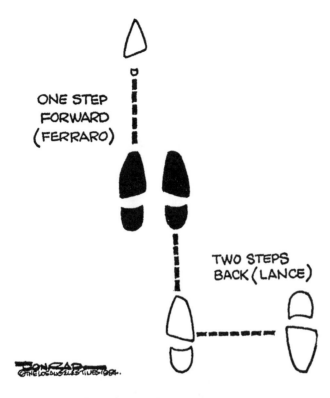

ONE STEP
FORWARD
(FERRARO)

TWO STEPS
BACK (LANCE)

## WHY MONDALE CAN'T DANCE

"LET'S FACE IT FRITZ...YOU'RE NO HARRY TRUMAN
AND I'M NO LAUREN BACALL!"

THEY JUST DON'T MAKE PRESIDENTS LIKE THEY USED TO

O THAT I WERE AS GREAT AS MY GRIEF, OR LESSER THAN MY NAME!
OR THAT I COULD FORGET WHAT I HAVE BEEN!
OR NOT REMEMBER WHAT I MUST BE NOW!

KING RICHARD II, ACT III, SCENE III

# FOR RICHER OR POORER

"IT'S A PRESIDENTIAL REPRIEVE!"

"HAVE A HEART!...ARTIFICIAL OR WHATEVER!"

"BLESS US, O LORD, AND THESE THY GIFTS WHICH WE ARE ABOUT
TO RECEIVE FROM WHAT IS LEFT OF OUR SOCIAL SECURITY CHECK..."

**THE OVERCROWDED LIFEBOAT**

DEUKMEJIAN'S COMMENCEMENT ADDRESS TO THE CLASS OF 1995

"OUTSIDE OF THAT, MOM, HOW DO YOU LIKE THE NURSING HOME?"

"NANCY, THIS ISN'T CALIFORNIA!"

"IN OTHER NEWS TODAY, 89% OF THE WORK FORCE IS NOT UNEMPLOYED…"

DEAFICIT

"MY CANDLE BURNS AT BOTH ENDS; IT WILL NOT LAST THE NIGHT; BUT, AH, MY FOES, AND, OH, MY FRIENDS—IT GIVES A LOVELY LIGHT."

—EDNA ST. VINCENT MILLAY

ONLY A WIZARD COULD HAVE
ARRANGED A DEFICIT SO LARGE
AS TO REQUIRE SUCH DRASTIC
CUTS IN DOMESTIC PROGRAMS...

...OR A DUNCE.

THE AMERICAN BANKING ASSOCIATION'S DRIVE-THRU WINDOW

"YOU DON'T LOOK TRULY NEEDY TO ME...
NEEDY PERHAPS, BUT NOT TRULY NEEDY!"

## "WE GOT THE MONEY! WE GOT THE MONEY!"

A favorite twist of the Conrad pen links global situations to oft-repeated television jingles. His target here was a Congressional giveaway of $8 billion to shore up U.S. bank loans to debt-ridden foreign countries.

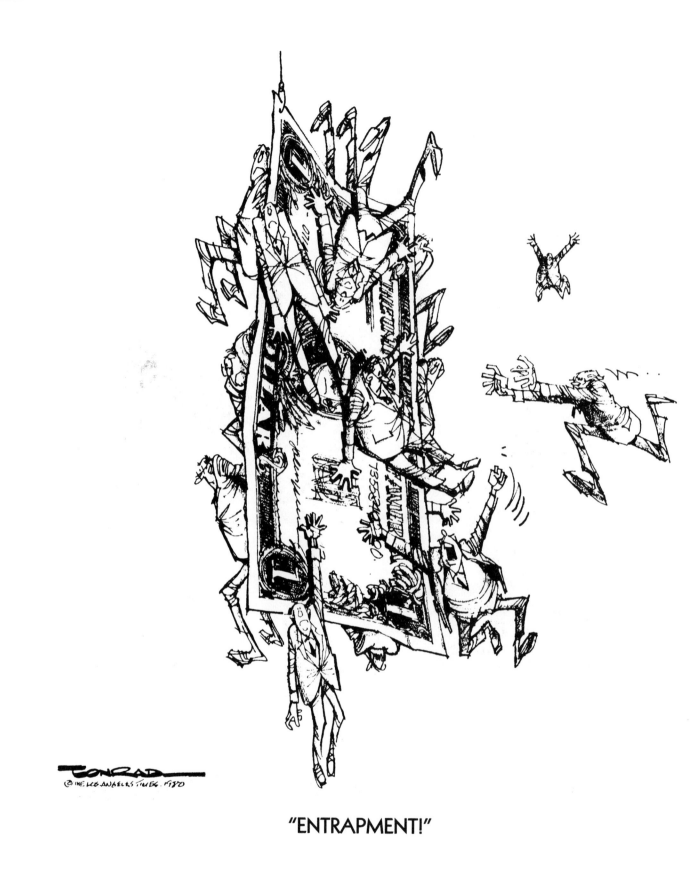

"ENTRAPMENT!"

In Conrad's view, good old greed may have been the real explanation for the "entrapment" alibi used by some U.S. congressmen accused of ABSCAM involvement.

**TRICKLE-DOWN THEORY**

RONALD REAGAN GOTHIC

The national deficit achieves human perspective with this visualization of a motorcyclist attempting to clear an endless row of barrels.

"IT ONLY HURTS WHEN REAGAN HOOD LAUGHS!"

REAGAN HOOD—HE TAKES FROM THE POOR
AND GIVES TO THE RICH!

"OK, EVERYBODY...SAY 'FREE CHEESE'!"

"BECAUSE OF OUR DEEPENING FINANCIAL PROBLEMS, THE U.S. HAS
DECLARED BANKRUPTCY UNDER CHAPTER 11 OF THE BANKRUPTCY CODE..."

*Dear Mr. Mondale —*
*Please accept my sincere apologies for heckling you during the past presidential campaign....*

REAGAN ADMINISTRATION TO CUT OR ELIMINATE STUDENT LOANS.

—NEWS ITEM

*Dere Sirs — As a Parunt I am asking you peeple their in the Nashunal Instatoot of Educashun why the basick Sckills of our Stoodence keeps going downwards when all the school are getting more dough than they no what too do with and us parunts is all the time beeing asked to support more tax increases after tax increases*

PREPARATIONS CONTINUE IN WASHINGTON FOR GALA INAUGURAL

## REFLECTIONS ON MRS. REAGAN'S NEW WHITE HOUSE CHINA

Outrage combined with compassion to provide this contrast of the bag lady's plight with the purchase of expensive White House china.

U.S. DECLARES VICTORY IN WAR ON POVERTY AND PULLS OUT.—NEWS ITEM

**SAFETY NET**

"THEN IT'S AGREED...YOU'LL TAKE CARE OF THE POOR
AND I'LL TAKE CARE OF THE RICH!"

"YOU SAY REGAN AND I SAY REAGAN; YOU SAY DEPRESSION AND I SAY RECESSION; REGAN-REAGAN-DEPRESSION-RECESSION. LET'S CALL THE WHOLE THING OFF!"

**AFFIXING BLAME FOR OUR ECONOMIC PROBLEMS**

**PROSPERITY IS JUST AROUND THE CORNER**

# GUNS DON'T KILL PEOPLE...?

**FRIENDLY FIRE**

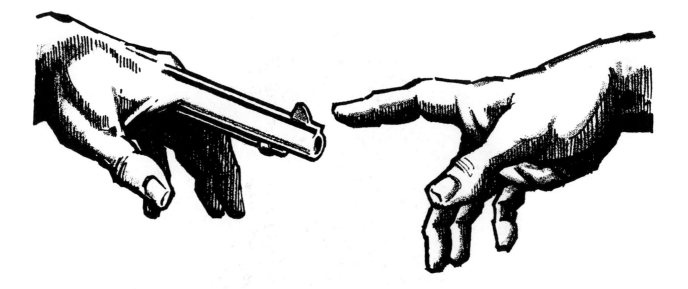

**IF GOD HAD MEANT MAN TO HAVE HANDGUNS...**

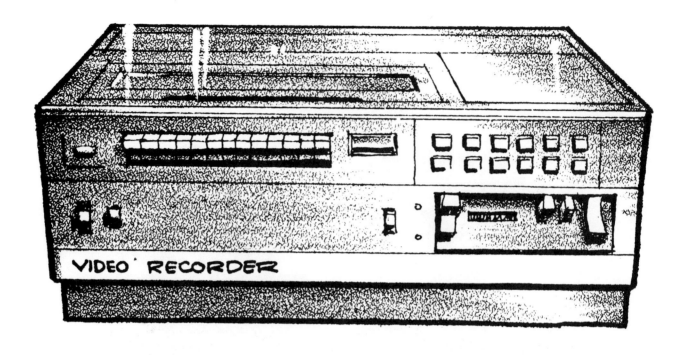

VIDEO RECORDER

ON WHICH ITEM HAVE THE COURTS RULED THAT MANUFACTURERS AND
RETAILERS BE HELD RESPONSIBLE FOR HAVING SUPPLIED THE EQUIPMENT?

## NRA PACIFIER

The National Rifle Association's childish resistance to proposed gun control regulations in California in 1982 was lampooned by Conrad.

# WE HAVE NOTHING TO FEAR
# BUT FEAR ITSELF

**BATTLESHIP NEW JERSEY RECOMMISSIONED.—NEWS ITEM**

I'VE NEVER SEEN A PURPLE COW.
I NEVER HOPE TO SEE ONE.
BUT I CAN TELL YOU, ANYHOW.
I'D RATHER SEE THAN B-1.

COMING UP...ONE WEINBERGER—WITH EVERYTHING

"I'M WILLING TO DISCUSS THE ARMS RACE WHENEVER THOSE RUSSIAN DEVILS ARE!"

"NOW THAT WE'VE AGREED ON REDUCTION OF WARHEADS, LET'S TALK ABOUT MISSILES."

AFTER ALL, WHAT ARE MOTHERS FOR?

**REMOVING ANOTHER NUCLEAR WAR HEAD**

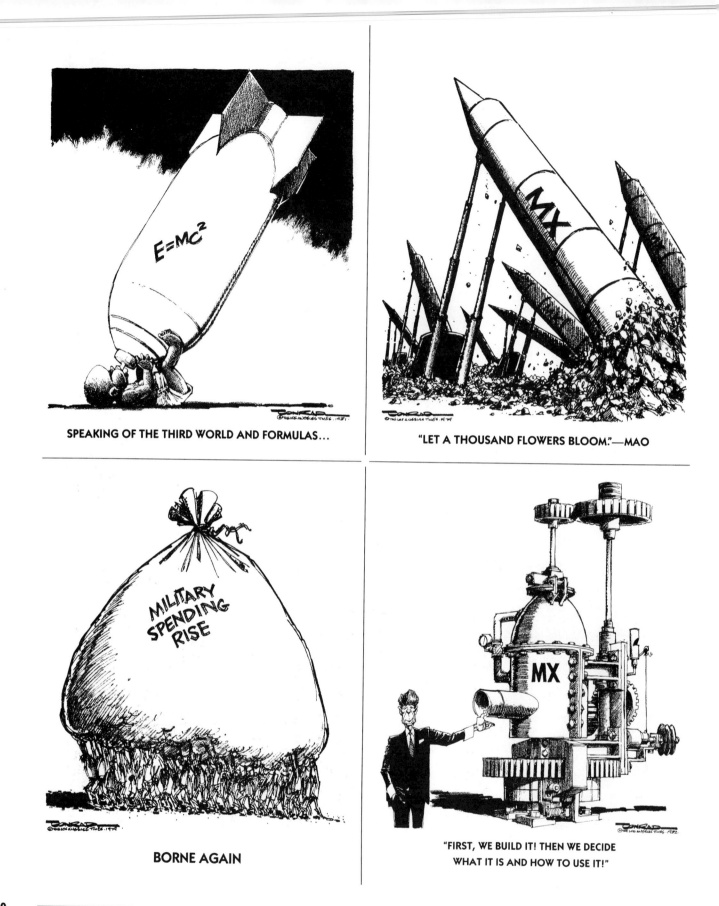

SPEAKING OF THE THIRD WORLD AND FORMULAS...

"LET A THOUSAND FLOWERS BLOOM."—MAO

BORNE AGAIN

"FIRST, WE BUILD IT! THEN WE DECIDE
WHAT IT IS AND HOW TO USE IT!"

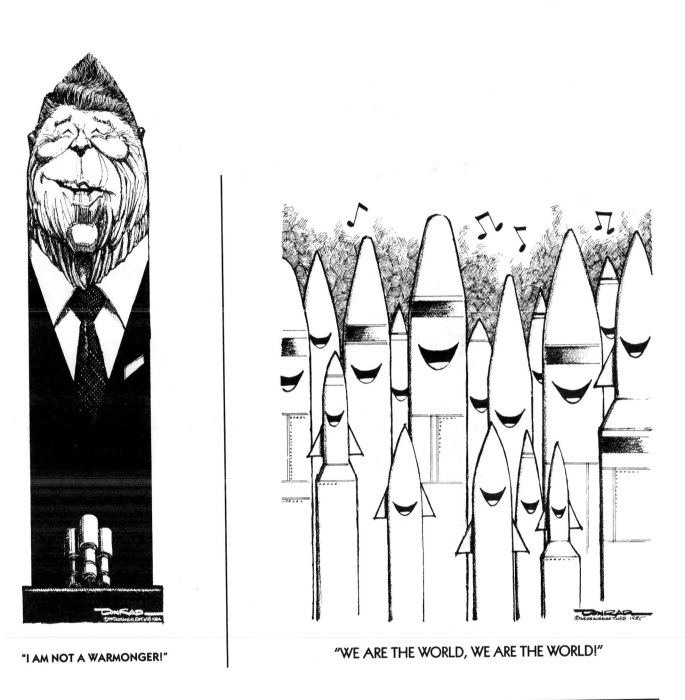

"I AM NOT A WARMONGER!"

"WE ARE THE WORLD, WE ARE THE WORLD!"

**QUESTION: WHICH OF THESE VEHICLES HAS MORE BOLTS
HOLDING ITS ENGINE ON?**

The VW bug, once a favored transport for Conrad, achieved better marks for engineering than the troubled DC-10 when it was under investigation for losing an engine in a 1979 fatal crash.

"WELL, TELL HIM TO TURN UP HIS HEARING AID!"

Playing off on news that President Reagan used a hearing aid, Conrad focused attention on his deafness to pleas that Marines be removed from Lebanon.

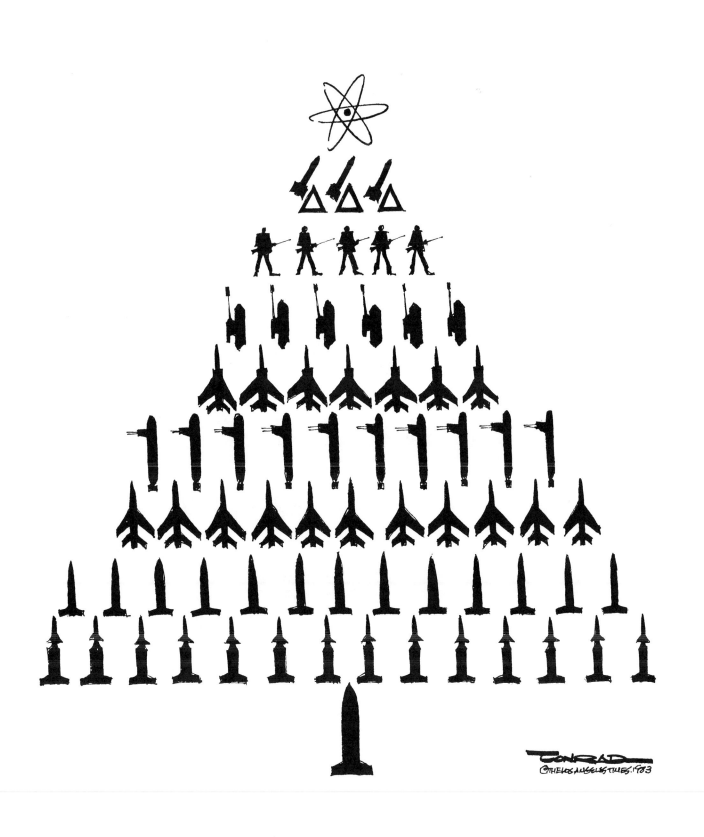

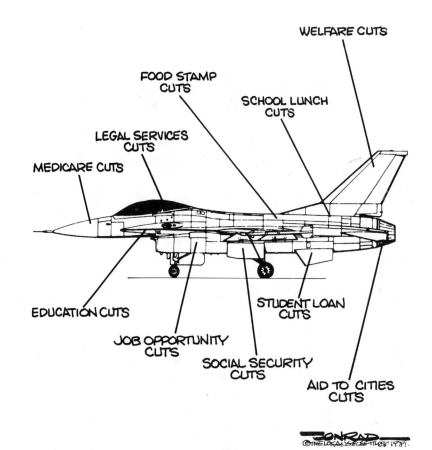

WELFARE CUTS

FOOD STAMP
CUTS

SCHOOL LUNCH
CUTS

LEGAL SERVICES
CUTS

MEDICARE CUTS

EDUCATION CUTS

STUDENT LOAN
CUTS

JOB OPPORTUNITY
CUTS

SOCIAL SECURITY
CUTS

AID TO CITIES
CUTS

CONRAD
©THE LOS ANGELES TIMES 1981

# ...CERTAIN UNALIENABLE RIGHTS

HUMAN RITES

ONE GIANT STEP FOR WOMANKIND

"I THINK I KNOW WHY WE'VE NEVER HAD A WOMAN ON THE TICKET!"

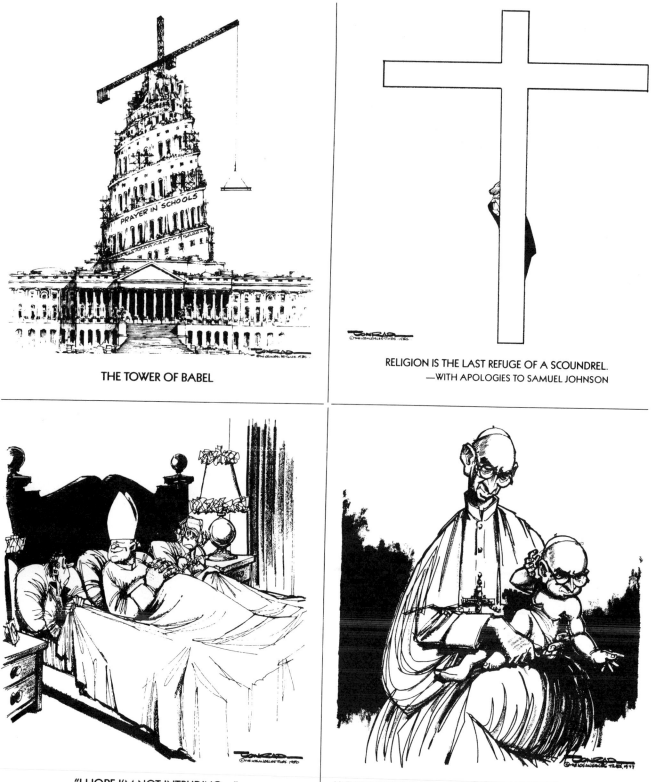

THE TOWER OF BABEL

RELIGION IS THE LAST REFUGE OF A SCOUNDREL.
—WITH APOLOGIES TO SAMUEL JOHNSON

"I HOPE I'M NOT INTRUDING..."

VATICAN PROHIBITS ORDINATION OF WOMEN AS PRIESTS BECAUSE
CHRIST'S REPRESENTATIVES MUST HAVE A NATURAL RESEMBLANCE TO HIM.
—NEWS ITEM

"DID SHE MENTION WOMEN?"

"WHY CAN'T A WOMAN BE MORE LIKE A MAN?
MEN ARE SO HONEST, SO THOROUGHLY SQUARE,
ETERNALLY NOBLE, HISTORICALLY FAIR;
WHO, WHEN YOU WIN, WILL ALWAYS GIVE YOUR BACK A PAT—
WHY CAN'T A WOMAN BE MORE LIKE THAT?"

"BUT PUT A WOMAN ON THE COURT! THEY'RE SUCH AN INDEPENDENT SORT!
SHE'LL VOTE FOR WOMEN'S CHOICES—WITH THEIR SHRILL AND SQUEAKY VOICES.
IF YOU EVER PUT A WOMAN ON THE COURT!"

"SEXISM, HELL! WE DID THE SAME THING TO EARL WARREN!"

As far back as 1978 conservatives attempted to frustrate the state supreme court reelection of California Chief Justice Rose Bird, and Conrad saw her then, as now, as a wronged Joan of Arc.

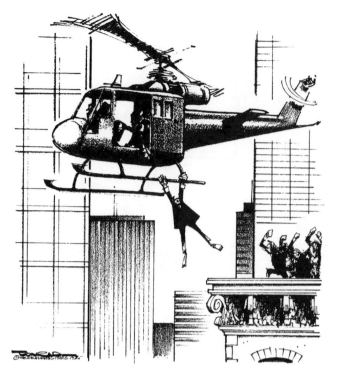

WESTMORELAND DECLARES VICTORY OVER CBS AND PULLS OUT

"GOVERNOR DEUKMEJIAN, YOU ARE CHARGED WITH VETOING
THE STRIP AND SEARCH BILL…PLEASE BEND OVER…"

"OH, EXCUSE ME, MA'AM...I MUST BE IN THE WRONG GHETTO!"

BLACK TEEN-AGERS 40% UNEMPLOYED. — NEWS ITEM

"WE'RE LOW ON WHITE..."

This cartoon exposes the tragic irony when police killed a black woman in Los Angeles, distraught because her gas service was cut off when she could not pay a utility bill. Her name—Eulia Love.

**CUSTER'S REVENGE**

EXPERIMENTAL ANIMALS

Conrad adds a new link to the evolutionist chain of mankind progressing from ape to higher forms of life.

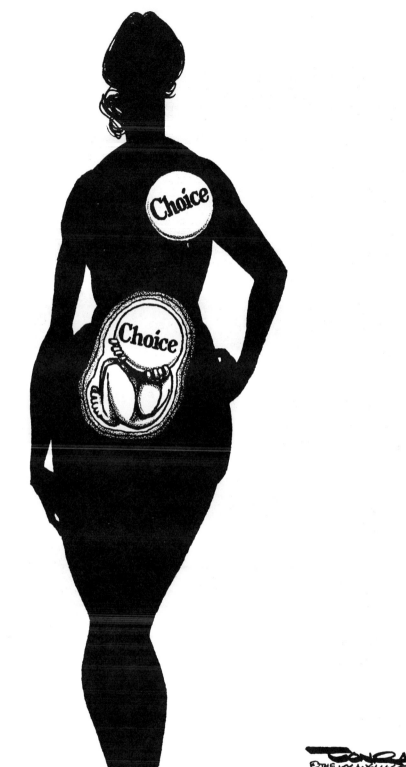

"YOU DON'T HAVE A RESERVATION AND YOU DON'T QUALIFY FOR FOOD STAMPS OR WELFARE. BUT, HERE'S A BROCHURE FOR AVOIDING ADOLESCENT PREGNANCY AND PARENTHOOD!"

FORGIVE THEM, FATHER, FOR THEY KNOW NOT WHAT THEY DO...

THE WRITING ON THE WALL IN THE OLD FOLKS HOME

"YOU'RE ON YOUR OWN, KID, ONCE YOU'RE BORN!"

SPEAKING OF AMERICAN CULTS...

"I DON'T KNOW ANYTHING ABOUT ART, BUT I KNOW WHAT I LIKE...!"

Offended by a *Los Angeles Times* review of his work, an artist sent a truckload of manure to be dumped at the door of the newspaper, and Artist Conrad sympathized with this response.

## ABORTION WARD

"I'M SORRY TO HAVE TO TELL YOU THIS, BUT
YOUR BABY WAS BORN LIVE."

SUPERBOWL

APARTHEID: A STUDY IN BLACK AND WHITE

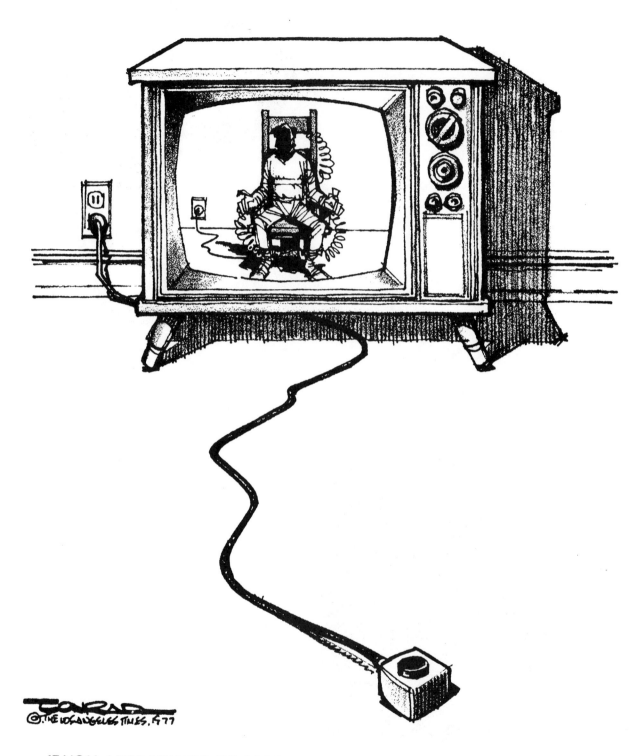

IF YOU ARE IN FAVOR OF CAPITAL PUNISHMENT, PUSH THIS BUTTON.

"RELIGION AND POLITICS ARE NECESSARILY RELATED."—REAGAN

The end of an ERA

# ALL THE WORLD'S A STAGE

THE EIGHTH WONDER OF THE WORLD

"THIS IS THE CAPTAIN SPEAKING: THIS IS A DISASTER,
BUT IT IS ALSO A GREAT OPPORTUNITY…"

THE CARTER BROTHERS' FOREIGN POLICY

'HELLO MUDDAH...HELLO FADDAH...HERE I AM AT...CAMP GRENADA...'

STANDING TALL

"HAVE I GOT A DEAL FOR YOU!"

"ANYONE THAT'S EVER HAD THEIR KITCHEN REMODELED KNOWS THAT
IT NEVER GETS DONE AS SOON AS YOU WISH IT WOULD."—REAGAN

Outrage can best describe Conrad's ridiculing of President Reagan's foolish, offhand defense
of the Pentagon's lapse of protection at the Marine barracks in Beirut, where 263 Americans
died in a terrorist attack.

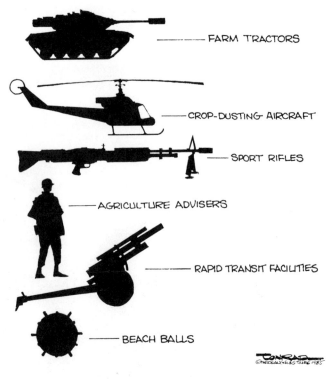

**U.S. ECONOMIC AID GUIDE TO CENTRAL AMERICA**

A possible repeat of U.S. involvement in Vietnam haunted Conrad when word emerged during the Ford administration of a CIA plan to embroil itself in the Angola situation.

"MOMMY, LOOK AT THE NICE PLANE!"

This poignant cartoon highlighted the plight of innocent persons killed when an unarmed Korean airliner was downed by Russian aircraft in 1983.

"THOSE RUSSIANS KILL **300** OF US AFGHANS AND NOBODY SAYS ANYTHING."

Responding again to the downing of a Korean airliner by Russian trackers, Conrad invited attention to the simultaneous lack of concern accompanying the Russian slaughter in Afghanistan.

THE DIFFERENCE BETWEEN 'OVERT' AND 'COVERT' C I A  MILITARY ACTIONS

"SOMEDAY, PRESIDENT THIEU, ALL THIS WILL BE YOURS!"

"PLAY IT AGAIN, RON..."

## FLAG RAISING AT GUANTANAMO

Conrad's unexcelled knack for parody vaulted the Marx Brothers into starring roles after a chest-thumping U.S. exercise at Guantanamo naval base in Cuba, taking off on the famous World War II photograph of the marine flag raising at Iwo Jima.

PRESIDENT REAGAN'S TEFLON SUIT

AND THEY SHALL BEAT THEIR PLOWS INTO MISSILESHARES...

"WHO THE HELL IS MIKHAIL GORBACHEV?"

BOAT PEOPLE

'VICTORY FINDS A HUNDRED FATHERS

—DEFEAT IS AN ORPHAN'

NAMES NOT LISTED ON THE VIETNAM WAR MEMORIAL

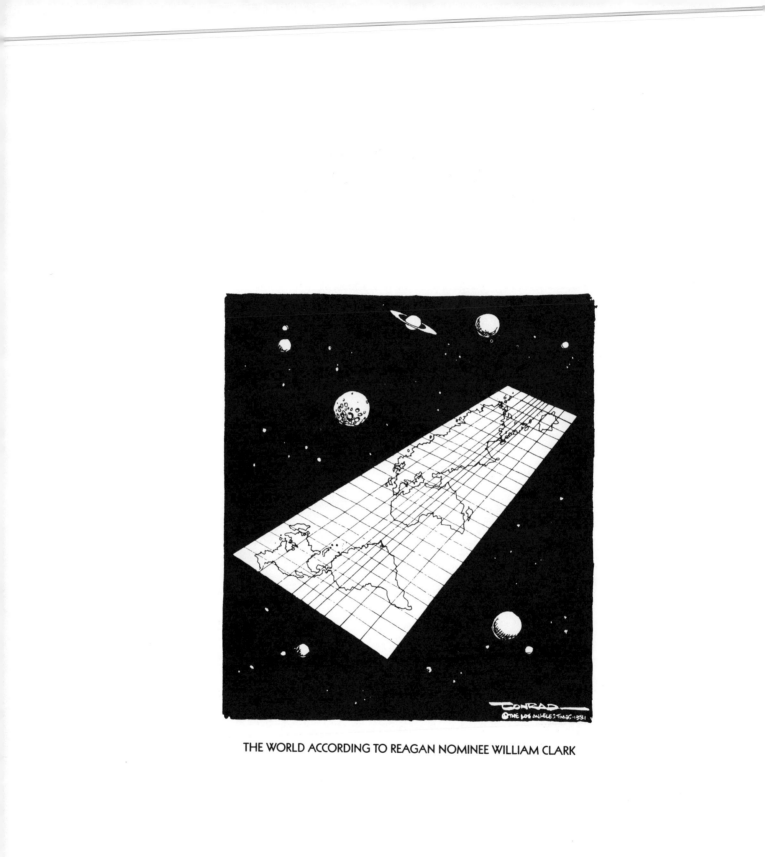

THE WORLD ACCORDING TO REAGAN NOMINEE WILLIAM CLARK

# FANFARES AND FAREWELLS

"GOOD NIGHT, JIMMY DURANTE...WHEREVER YOU ARE..."

**SGT. PEPPER'S LONELY HEARTS CLUB BAND**
It was twenty years ago today,
Sgt. Pepper taught the band to play
They've been going in and out of style
But they're guaranteed to raise a smile.
So may I introduce to you
The act you've known for all these years,
Sgt. Pepper's Lonely Hearts Club Band.
We're Sgt. Pepper's Lonely Hearts Club
Band,
We hope you will enjoy the show,
We're Sgt. Pepper's Lonely Hearts Club
Band,
Sit back and let the evening go.
Sgt. Pepper's lonely, Sgt. Pepper's lonely,
Sgt. Pepper's Lonely Hearts Club Band.
It's wonderful to be here,
It's certainly a thrill.
You're such a lovely audience,
We'd like to take you home with us,
We'd love to take you home.
I don't really want to stop the show,
But I thought that you might like to
know,
That the singer's going to sing a song,
And he wants you all to sing along.
So let me introduce to you
The one and only Billy Shears
And Sgt. Pepper's Lonely Hearts Club
Band.

**A LITTLE HELP FROM MY FRIENDS**
A little help from my friends,
What would you think if I sang out of
tune,
Would you stand up and walk out on me
Lend me your ears and I'll sing you a
song,
And I'll try not to sing out of key.
I get by with a little help from my friends,
I get high with a little help from my
friends,
Going to try with a little help from my
friends.
What do I do when my love is away.
(Does it worry you to be alone)
How do I feel by the end of the day
(Are you sad because you're on your own)
No I get by with a little help from my
friends,
Do you need anybody
I need somebody to love.
Could it be anybody
I want somebody to love.
Would you believe in a love at first sight,
Yes I'm certain that it happens all the
time.
What do you see when you turn out the
light,
I can't tell you, but I know it's mine.

That grow so incredibly high.
Newspaper taxis appear on the shore,
Waiting to take you away.
Climb in the back with your head in the
clouds,
And you're gone.
Lucy in the sky with diamonds,
Picture yourself on a train in a station,
With Plasticine porters with looking
glass ties,
Suddenly someone is there at the
turnstile,
The girl with the kaleidoscope eyes.

**GETTING BETTER**
It's getting better all the time
I used to get mad at my school
The teachers that taught me weren't cool
You're holding me down, turning me
round
Filling me up with your rules.
I've got to admit it's getting better
A little better all the time
I have to admit it's getting better
It's getting better since you've been mine.
Me used to be a angry young man
Me hiding me head in the sand
You gave me the word
I finally heard
I'm doing the best that I can
I've got to admit it's getting better
I used to be cruel to my woman
I beat her and kept her apart from the
things that she loved
Man I was mean but I'm changing my
scene
And I'm doing the best that I can
I admit it's getting better
A little better all the time
Yes I admit it's getting better
It's getting better since you've been mine.

**FIXING A HOLE**
I'm fixing a hole where the rain gets in
And stops my mind from wandering
Where it will go
I'm filling the cracks that ran through
the door
And kept my mind from wandering
Where it will go
And it really doesn't matter if I'm wrong
I'm right
Where I belong I'm right
Where I belong.
See the people standing there who
disagree and never win
And wonder why they don't get in my door.
I'm painting my room in a
colourful way
And when my mind is wandering
There I will go.

For so many years. Bye, bye
Father snores as his wife gets into her
dressing gown
Picks up the letter that's lying there
Standing alone at the top of the stairs
She breaks down and cries to her husband
Daddy our baby's gone.
Why would she treat us so thoughtlessly
How could she do this to me.
She  (We never thought of ourselves)
is leaving  (Never a thought for ourselves)
home  (We struggled hard all
        our lives to get by)
She's leaving home after living alone
For so many years. Bye, Bye
Friday morning at nine o'clock she is far
away
Waiting to keep the appointment she
made
Meeting a man from the motor trade.
She    What did we do that was wrong
is having  We didn't know it was wrong
fun    Fun is the one thing that
        money can't buy
Something inside that was always denied
For so many years. Bye, Bye
She's leaving home bye bye

**BEING FOR THE BENEFIT OF MR. KITE!**
For the benefit of Mr. Kite
There will be a show tonight on
trampoline
The Hendersons will all be there
Late of Pablo Fanques fair, what a scene
Over men and horses hoops and garters
Lastly through a hogshead of real fire!
In this way Mr. K. will challenge the
world!
The celebrated Mr. K.
performs his feat on Saturday at
Bishopsgate
The Hendersons will dance and sing
As Mr. Kite flys through the ring don't
be late
Messrs. K and H assure the public
Their production will be second to none
And of course Henry The Horse dances
the waltz!
The band begins at ten to six
When Mr. K. performs his tricks without
a sound
And Mr. H. will demonstrate
Ten somersets he'll undertake on
solid ground
Having been some days in preparation
A splendid time is guaranteed for all
And tonight Mr. Kite is topping the bill.
John Lennon & Paul McCartney

On the medal:
24K
XXIII
OLYMPIAD
LOS ANGELES
1984

CONRAD
© THE LOS ANGELES TIMES 1984

"BARNEY CLARK...YOU'RE 112 DAYS LATE!"

John Wayne's grit during his battle against recurring cancer (the big C) was depicted as true heroics.

WE THE PEOPLE

# I N T E R V I E W

Paul Conrad is a creator. His job is to look at the news and convert his opinions into a pictorial jab—or haymaker. He uses satire to poke fun at the human condition. But most of all, he uses his pen to send the world a message. And the clearer the message, the better he has done his job.

But when you ask Conrad how he creates, what formula or process he uses to convert the printed word into a pictorial message, his simple answer is "I read a lot."

*Everywhere you go, people want to know where you get your ideas for cartoons. What do you tell them?*

First there's an association that goes on in this computer here (pointing to his head). The only way you feed that computer is by reading, as far as I'm concerned. Reading, reading, reading. And this computer (again pointing to his head) stores magnificently. If a news story breaks, I recall what happened the last time in a similar situation.

*How do you know your memory is infallible?*

Oh, I know it's not. I get a suggestion out of my built-in computer and I think, now wait a minute, am I right on this? So I call the [*Times*] library and say, give me the clips on such and such—a date, a quote, whatever. In fifteen minutes it's here in my office.

*So you get your facts checked?*

Right. You've got to go with the facts.

*Normally, you draw your cartoons by early afternoon for the following day's newspaper. How does it all get started?*

I read the *Times,* the first two sections at least, when I get up in the morning. Kay [Mrs. Conrad] and I discuss the news.

*Do her views mesh pretty well with yours?*

They sure do. As a matter of fact, if you think I'm radical, you should hear her! Particularly on economics. She thinks this whole Reaganomics thing is absolute nonsense. You see, she's on the board of directors of Little Company of Mary Hospital and has been working with school districts. She's seen first-hand the damage Reaganomics is doing.

REAGAN'S OLIVE BRANCH TO NICARAGUA

*Does that affect your ultimate opinion?*

It reinforces mine.

*So when you come to work every day, you have at least a running jump on what's in the news. Do you watch TV in the morning?*

No. But I listen to news radio and talk radio on the long drive to work. And when I get to the office, I have access to all the editorial people and the computers and the daily news file, so I get a grasp on what's going to be in the paper the next day. And I try to match a news story with an opinion on it on the Op-Ed page.

*Let's take an example. Here's the cartoon you did on Reagan's so-called peace plan for Nicaragua, an olive branch with bombs for leaves. How did you arrive at that?*

I read the story in which Reagan was quoted as saying that a vote against his plan for $14 million in aid to the contras would literally be a vote against peace. Well, that's absolute non-sense! I checked other stories and all had the same quote. But I've done many cartoons on the Central American situation. How could I do it differently? It just occurred to me, turn the leaves into bombs, because this is what an olive branch means to Reagan—take my peace offer or I'll blow your head off.

*You roughed it out first?*

Oh yes, I always do. And I took the rough and showed it around to some of the people in this part of the building, just to get their reactions.

*I remember when you first came here more than twenty years ago, you circulated your roughs to a group including me. And I quickly concluded that you really didn't give a damn about what I said about your idea, your message. You just wanted to see what happened to my face. If it lit up instantly, you knew you had a winner. But if there was a long, studied examination, you probably weren't thrilled.*

Yes. If I have to explain what I'm trying to say, I'd better start over.

*But roughs can be exceedingly rough, just some quick lines on a piece of scratch paper.*

That's true. I draw just enough so I can get the idea down, just enough for people to understand where I'm going. And if I have to explain it, well, there's always a way, if you're really stuck. There's always a way to simplify. And if it still doesn't work, go on to something else. But if simplification has helped, then that's the way to go.

*The basic rule then is the simpler the better?*

Simplification is the key, because people aren't interested in all the words and the rest of it. I hate balloons [quotes encapsulated in lines] in cartoons. In fact, I'm not sure readers are that much interested in detailed, beautiful drawings. They want impact.

*Visual impact or intellectual impact?*

Both. I've settled on a news story and I decide this is the way I want to go in my cartoon message. Now I'm looking for a way to dramatize it, and I recall a quote, a word, a drawing, whatever gives me the key.

*You're the ultimate judge as to whether it works or not. When you show the roughs around, do you get to the point where you're simply reinforcing what you have already decided?*

No, I'm showing them just to make sure that what I'm trying to say is said in this drawing. You want to know if the guy in the street, the ordinary person, will understand it.

*Sometimes you start with one way of making your point, and wind up with a totally different one. Let's talk about examples of this.*

All right. When Reagan announced he was going to visit the German cemetery in Bitburg last May, I thought it was stupid and utterly insensitive. And so my first rough showed an American cemetery and one GI was speaking from the grave to another and saying, "I understand Reagan is going to send Dr. Mengele to honor us GIs." But there's a problem. How many know who Mengele is? The message was just too vague. So I figured it had to go right to Reagan. Through the figures of Willie and Joe, from the Bill Mauldin cartoons of World War II, I was able to do that—carry the thing one step further and say that if Reagan's not going to visit a concentration camp site, he ought to go the full route and lay a wreath at Hitler's bunker. And that's how I wound up with the Willie and Joe cartoon.

*Did you do a rough of the Mengele idea and show it around?*

Yes, but I knew it wasn't going to fly. Actually, there are a lot of times when you really have to draw something like that and get it out of your system, and have someone tell you, no, it doesn't work. Because I'm not sure the mind's eye always tells you the right thing about what you're seeing.

**169**

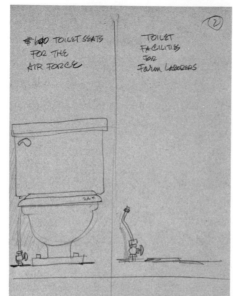

THE KILLING FIELDS

*The Willie and Joe thing makes contact with people who remember Mauldin and World War II. A lot of your readers weren't even born then. Don't you risk losing part of your audience?*

I think most people today have been exposed to Mauldin's characters, either by having seen them at the time or having seen them in history books. And there have been a lot of World War II movies. But if the reader has not been reading, does not know current events, does not know history, that's his problem, not mine. I don't think I lost many on that cartoon.

*You were greatly upset when Reagan said the contras in Nicaragua were freedom fighters, the moral equivalents of our founding fathers.*

That to me was just insane. So I did several roughs on this. The first showed a little, Napoleon-type guy, and Reagan had his arm around him, making that statement. Well, it was static. It just didn't go anywhere. And then I did another rough of a guerrilla type, the moral equivalent of our founding fathers. Nothing. Then I drew a group of contras crossing some water and shooting people and bayoneting floating bodies. I used the same poses as the famous painting of Washington crossing the Delaware. But it didn't seem to work either.

*Did you show it around?*

Yeah, but I wasn't sold on it. It wasn't right to the point. Finally, I thought of Mt. Rushmore and the presidents there and thought about Reagan's statement about the founding fathers and the contras. So I had Washington talking to Jefferson saying, "Mr. Jefferson, were you ever accused of rape, murder, kidnapping, torture, and mutilation?" as some of the contras have been accused. In the final drawing, I had Jefferson responding, "Not until now." Later, a reader sent in the cartoon on which he had written another statement from Jefferson: "But I did buy and sell slaves." Marvelous. It's amazing what readers see in some of the cartoons.

*I remember you were outraged when the Reagan administration refused to issue orders requiring farmers to provide sanitation facilities for farm workers. And you eventually wound up with a cartoon based on the movie "The Killing Fields." The tie-in with the movie title is obvious, but how did you progress from roughs to final drawing in that case?*

Well, I hadn't seen the movie, but I'd heard it was good. But that wasn't where I started. I wanted to show that the lack of sanitation facilities, which the federal government had ruled employers did not have to supply, was actually killing people with dysentery; that it was impossible to wash off the pesticides when working in the fields all day; and that the workers should be allowed to clean themselves, and so on.

First, because the farm workers weren't even provided with toilets, and it had been reported at about the same time that the Air Force was paying $640 for toilet seats, I framed a picture of farm workers through a toilet seat and had them saying, "We don't want $640 toilet seats like the Air Force, all we want is a toilet." Well, I thought that idea was too focused on the $640 toilet seat rather than on the farm workers' problem.

So then I went to a split cartoon, showing a toilet with a 24-karat gold seat on one side, and the farm workers without facilities on the other side. But once again, the cartoon got lost on the Air Force toilet seat instead of dealing with the farm workers.

The third attempt was one showing the farm workers out in the field; one of them is saying, "If the Air Force can pay $640 for toilet seats, why can't we just get a toilet?" And another guy answers, "Join the Air Force."

But I was still stuck on the Air Force thing. So then I went to "The Killing Fields." I don't know how I thought of it. I guess it just happened. I got the logo, the poster for the movie, out of an ad in the paper, and just changed it around a little, with a shower and faucet and an "Out of Order" sign, labeling it "Farm Worker Sanitation Facilities." These truly were the killing fields. Now this drawing got back solely to the plight of the farm workers. But the progression of roughs to the final cartoon shows an important point, that a cartoonist really has to care about a situation that government does absolutely nothing about, and not get lost on the details such as the cost of a toilet seat.

*Which brings up the question, what do you consider the function of an editorial cartoonist to be?*

I believe it is to speak for the people in this country, in some cases the world, who have no voice. In so doing, the cartoonist has to be as informed as possible. That's why all the reading is required. A cartoonist has to care very deeply about the issues confronting the nation and the world. I'm not certain that any cartoonist has ever solved anything, but I think we help in clarifying the issues and providing a voice for the common folk who don't have a forum.

*So what you're doing is putting yourself in the shoes of the quote ordinary man unquote?*

Absolutely.

*How can you do that when you're not an ordinary person?*

I think I am. I know I am...therefore, I am!

*Your training, your education, your talents, they're anything but ordinary. Obviously you make more money, you have a far different life-style. What makes you think you're ordinary?*

Because—Jesus, that's a terrible question. I feel that I am an ordinary guy. I care about the same problems. That's more than I can say for many of our elected officials. And I would like justice done in so many cases. The only means that I have, the only talent I have, is to express those concerns and problems to those who, I would hope, can do something about them.

*You're presenting your views from the standpoint of the ordinary man. You don't have to deal with the problems of meeting the costs of the changes you advocate. Would your viewpoint be different if you were the county supervisor, the governor, or the President? Is it possible that they, too, might care very deeply about some of the common man's problems, but say they simply don't have the money to solve them?*

Then the state, by God, should find the money. If I were a public official with the power to decide these issues, I would be ranting and raving to raise the dough and use it where necessary.

*You were taken off the editorial page in 1972 and moved to the Op-Ed page. Does that disturb you even now? How has it worked out?*

Everybody here denies that I was intentionally moved because of any particular cartoon or cartoons. I still think I was. I don't go to editorial conferences, but I am concerned about what positions the newspaper takes on issues. I think the move to Op-Ed was the best thing that ever happened, because now there's none of this nonsense about who speaks for the *Times*. And with the space created on the editorial page, we're getting more and better letters to the editor that we can publish. I think that's to everyone's advantage.

*Nevertheless, don't you occasionally peek at the page across from you and see what editorial positions the* Times *is taking?*

We agreed from Day One that if a cartoon works, isn't libelous, and is in good taste, so be it. This is "Ol' Con" talking, not the *Times*. But I don't recall having any major differences with the editorials other than on abortion. And I don't do many abortion cartoons anymore.

*Why not?*

Because the crazies have taken over the anti-abortion cause. The Pro-Lifers are bombing abortion clinics, and all the rest of it. I've had my say and I'm not sure that I can contribute anything more to the argument at this point.

*Your views haven't changed? You are still opposed to abortions, except in the case of rape and incest?*

That's right.

*People who know you're a devout Catholic must ask you if your position is based on your religion.*

They do, and it probably is. I'm not sure that all my views aren't based to some degree on my religion, my religious background, my social conscience.

*Has this been a point of puzzlement and controversy between you and your fans? So many will agree with you on almost everything you stand for until they come to your anti-abortion stand. Do they ask how such a fine, enlightened man such as you can take such an unintelligent view?*

Well, they're far kinder than that. Generally it goes like this: "Look, Con, I agree with you 98% of the time." I know immediately what the 2% is. And we just let it go at that.

"NICARAGUAN CONTRAS...
THE MORAL EQUIVALENT OF OUR FOUNDING FATHERS."—REAGAN

*You have a remarkable freedom in your work. You say you are bound mainly by matters of libel and taste. Let's take the question of taste. What is it, as it applies to cartooning?*

Well, I don't know how to define it. It's a lot like what a Supreme Court justice said about pornography, "I know it when I see it."

*Which brings to mind your famous cartoon (see page 25) of the Northern California man urinating on Southern California, after the northern part of the state overwhelmingly voted against a plan to bring excess water from the north to the central and southern parts of the state. Some of your readers were shocked by that. You didn't consider it in bad taste?*

Not at all. The facts bore out the cartoon. However, if I had drawn it from a different perspective, say from Arizona, then yes, that would have been bad taste.

*What do you mean?*

Well, if I had drawn it to show a frontal exposure, that would have been offensive.

*And when you drew the famous cartoon of former President Carter, who said he sometimes has lust in his heart, looking at a naked Statue of Liberty, was there a question of taste involved?*

I don't think that was bad taste at all. I had no problem with the readers on that. But taste is very hard to define. When I use slides in some of my talks, I show a rough drawing of four outhouses, all of them overturned. They're labeled "Mideast," "Balanced Budget," "Central America," and "The Deficit." Reagan is crawling out of one hole. Two men are standing nearby and one is saying, "Not to worry, he always comes out smelling like a rose."

*But that cartoon never saw the light of day. Why not?*

First, I think the taste is debatable. And second, in this day and age, how many readers know what an outhouse even looks like?

*Many editorial cartoonists rely heavily on humor, particularly satire. I know you do.*

You bet. In stating a proposition, you're always looking for the ludicrous aspects. Satire works in cartooning. For instance, the cartoon I did about Nancy Reagan's new White House china (see page 91). I thought it would be beautiful to show the china's design and then put the bag lady in the reflection to illustrate misplaced government spending and the lack of concern for one's fellow man, such as the cuts in the food stamp program.

*I suppose it's inevitable that sometimes you feel like the lord of the universe, expressing your opinions on a wide range of subjects, telling the world how it ought to behave. Does this lead to some kind of elitist arrogance?*

Oh no. I'm a very humble man (laughs). I really am. I think, quite frankly, that I'm only as good as tomorrow's cartoon. I've always felt that way. And that's why I work so very hard to try to do the best I can.

*You've won three Pulitzers, and just about all the other journalism awards there are. Wouldn't that make you a little less than humble?*

No, I think the awards, in fact, dictate humility. Each award, each Pulitzer, gets a little bit heavier, and then I try desperately to upgrade my work.

And there's one more thing. I'm a very lucky man. The fact that I get to come down here and draw—in space that's even set aside for me—is a forum very few have. The newspaper comes out every day. It's something special. I mean, if I were an engineer, or a car salesman, what outlet would I have for my opinions other than to scream at my wife, my neighbor, or my best friend? I have the forum. But most of all, I'm the ordinary man who happens to have a gift that is most necessary in creating editorial cartoons.

"FOUR MORE YEARS!"